Design Unique Cross Tattoos Like A Pro

Learn How To Design Unique Cross Tattoos

Cross Tattoos

By : Gala Publication

Published By :

Gala Publication
© Copyright 2015 – Gala Publication

ISBN-13: **978-1522707660**
ISBN-10: **1522707662**

Table of Contents

CELTIC CROSS
TATTOO

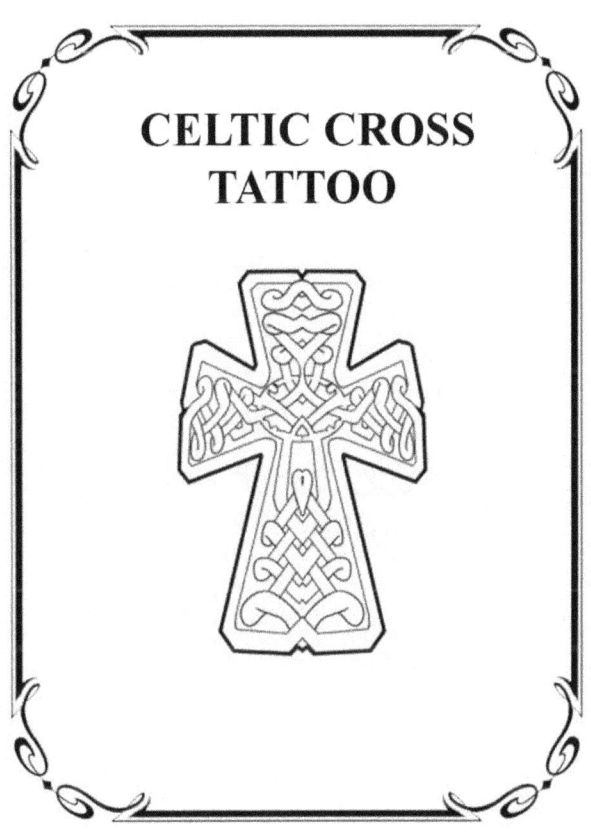

STEP 1

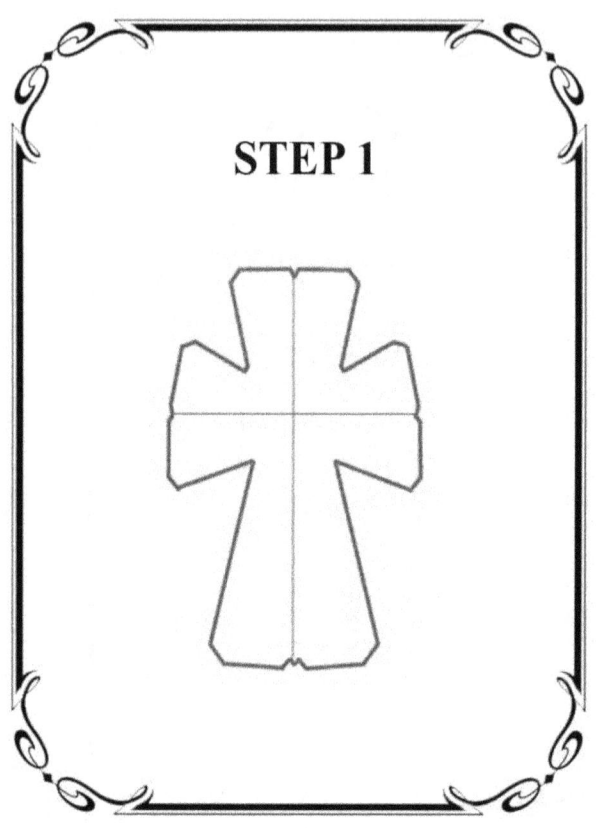

STEP 2

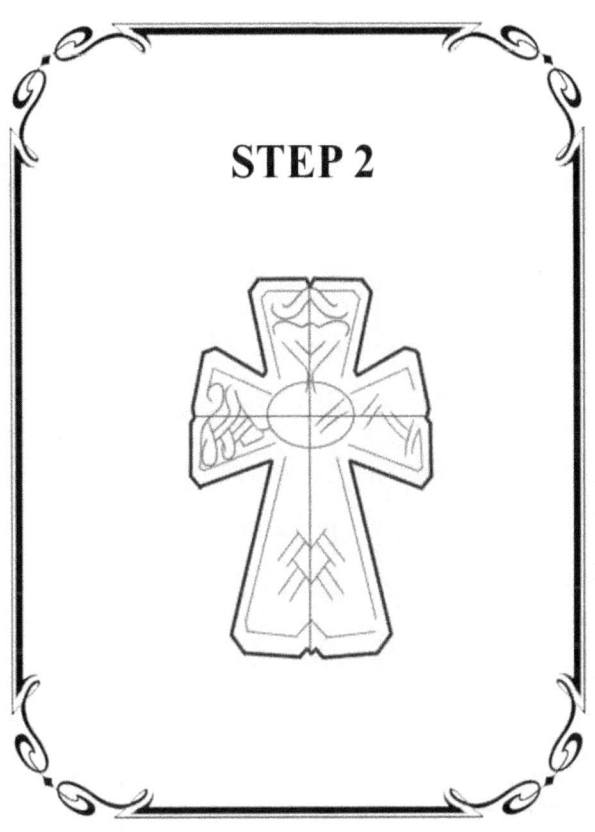

STEP 3

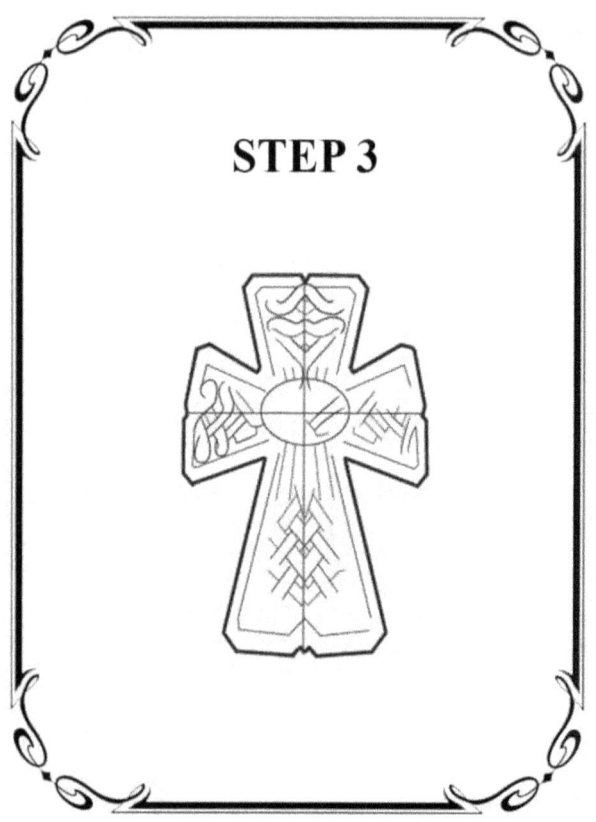

STEP 4

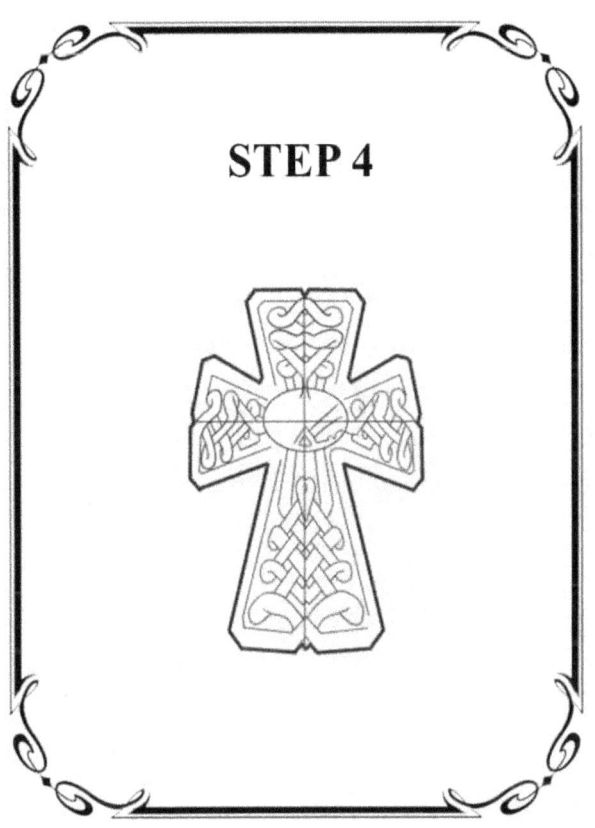

STEP 5

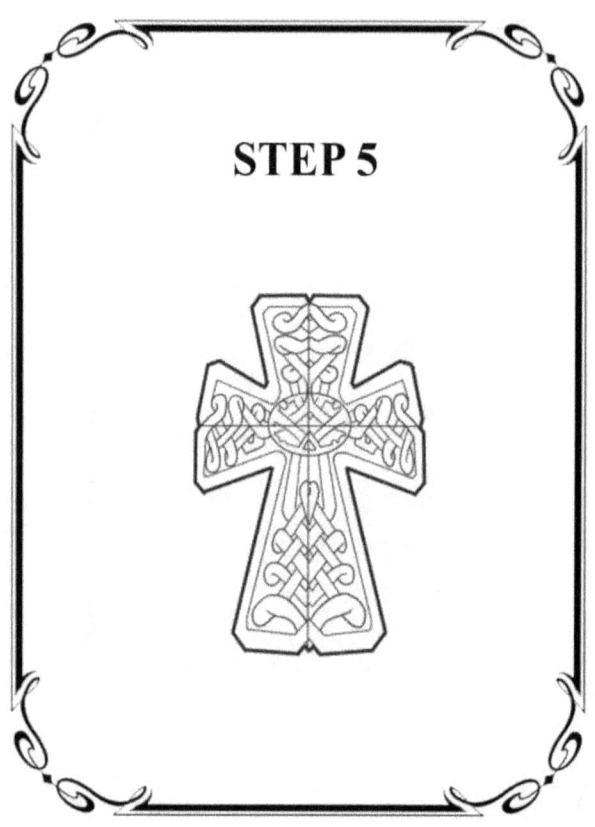

STEP 6

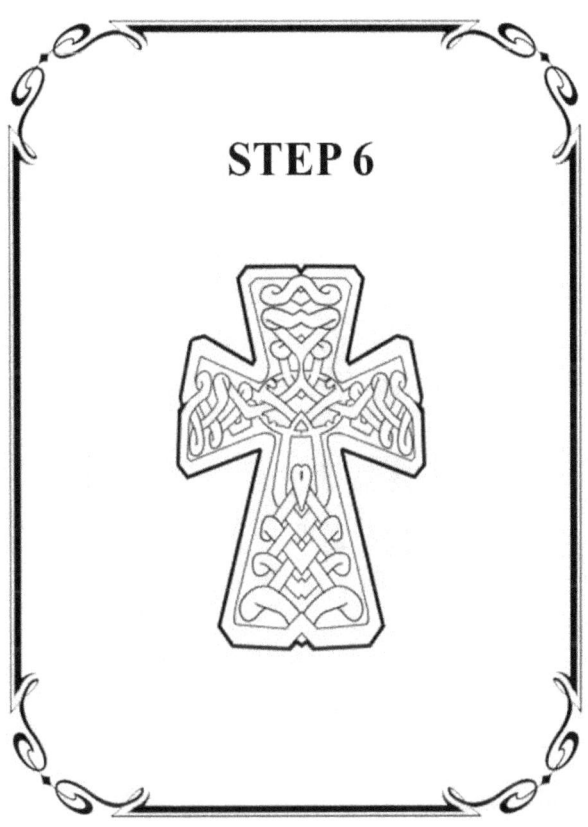

CROSS TATTOO

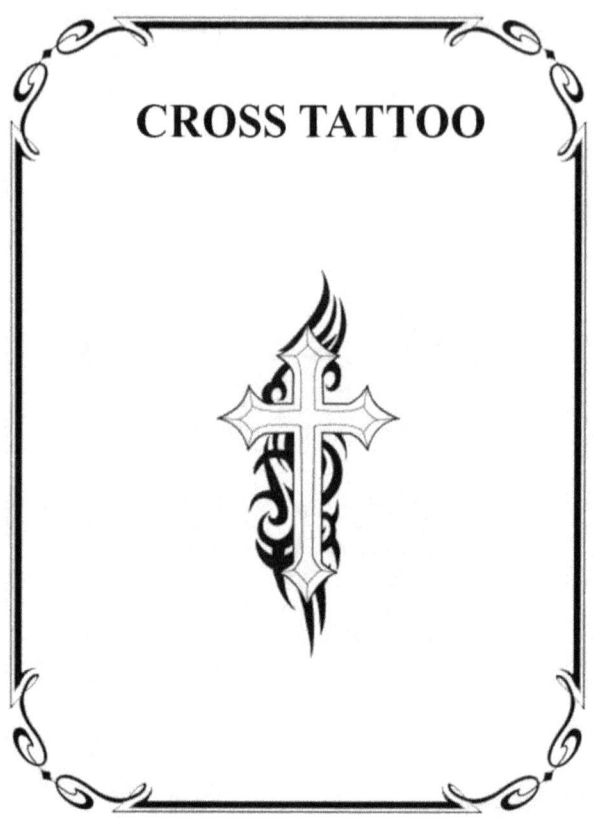

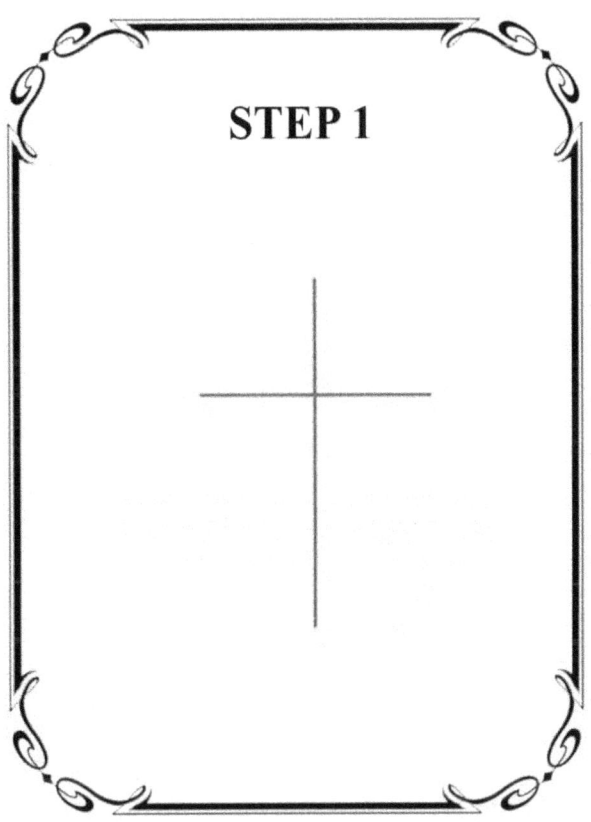

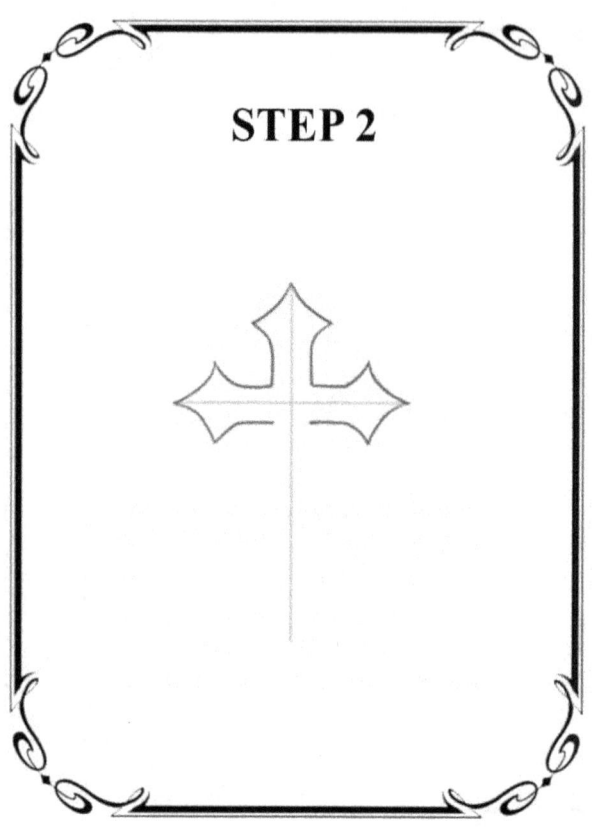

STEP 2

STEP 3

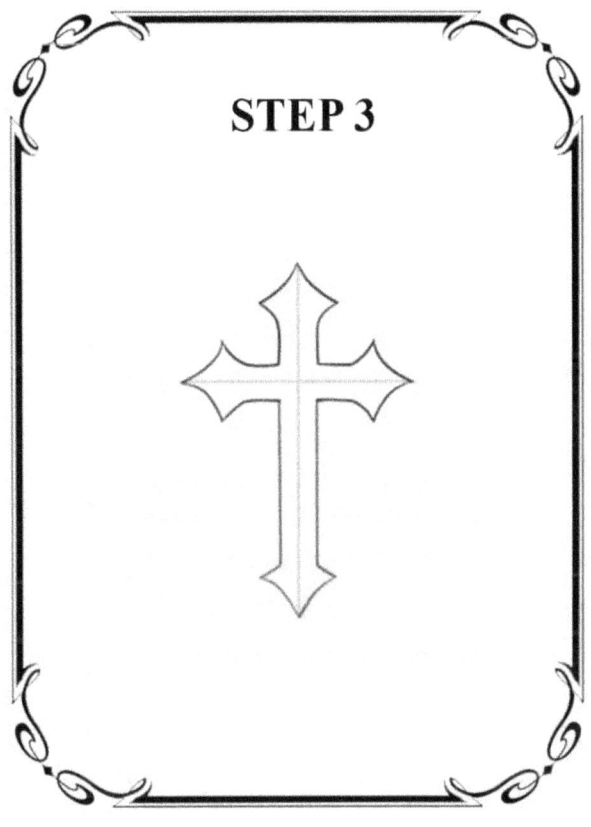

STEP 4

STEP 5

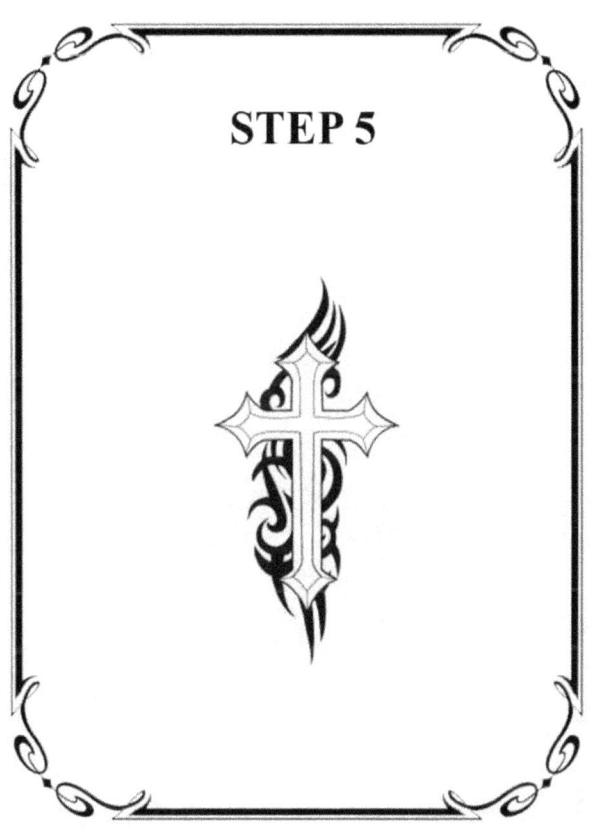

18

CRUCIFIX CROSS TATTOO

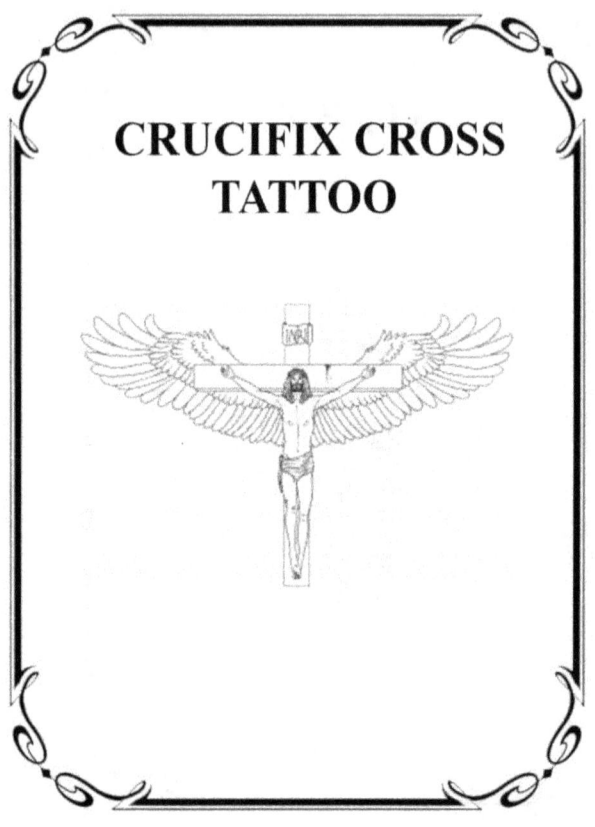

STEP 1

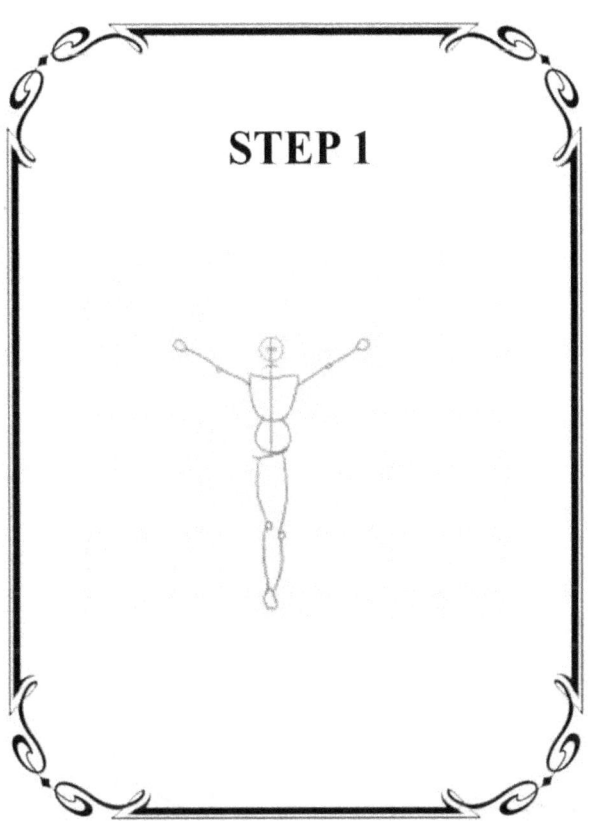

STEP 2

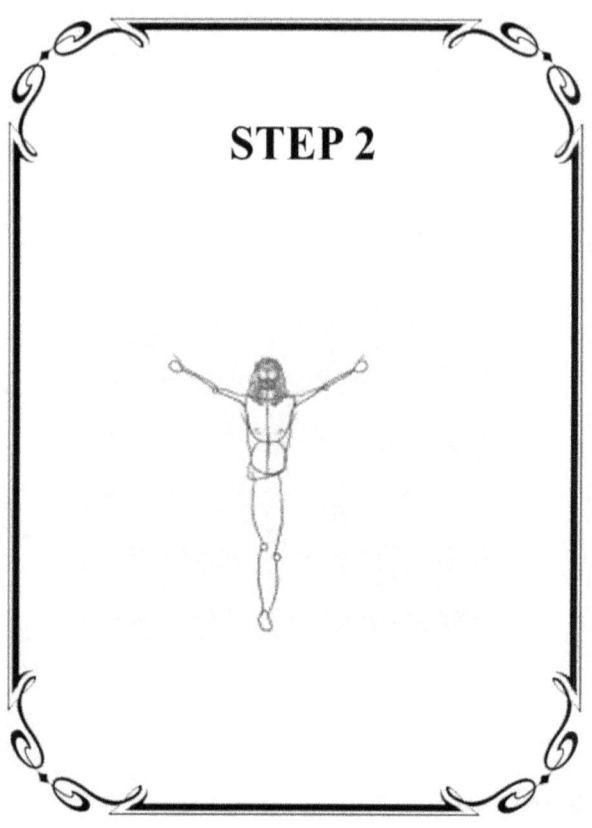

STEP 3

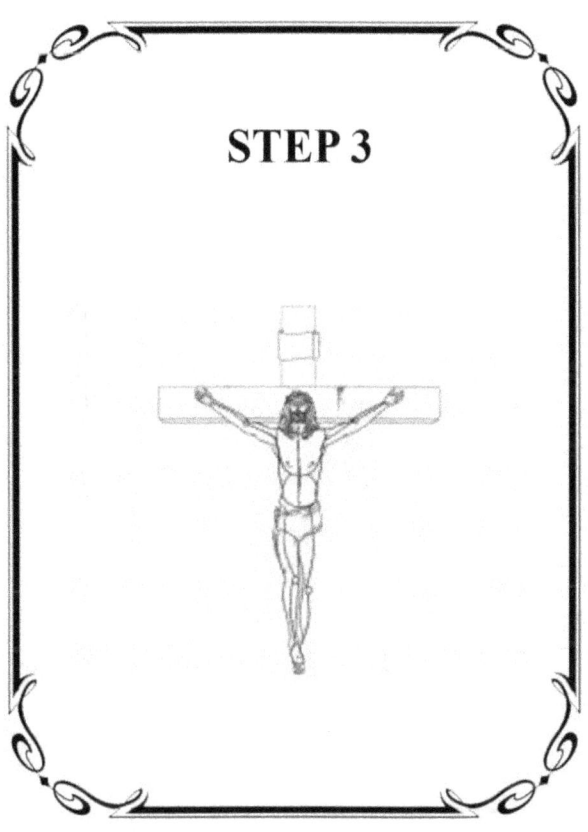

STEP 4

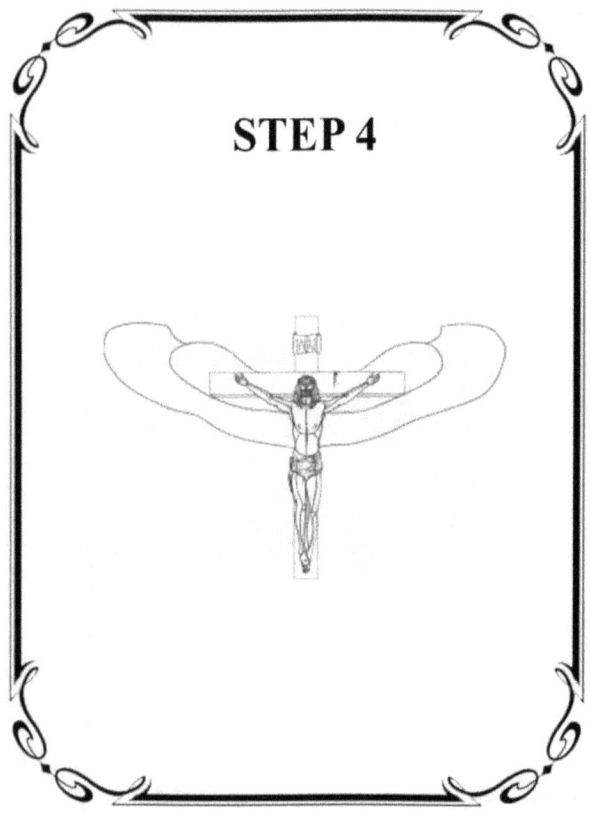

STEP 5

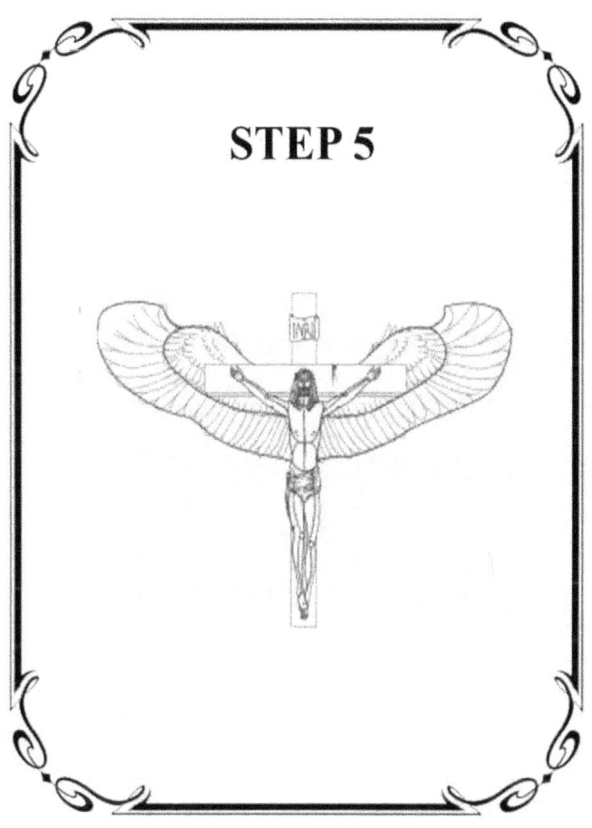

STEP 6

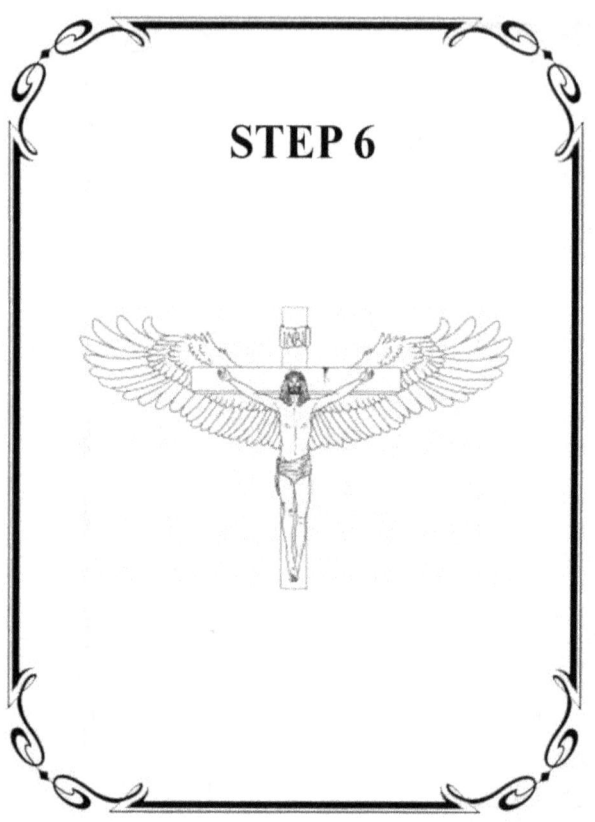

IRON CROSS
TATTOO

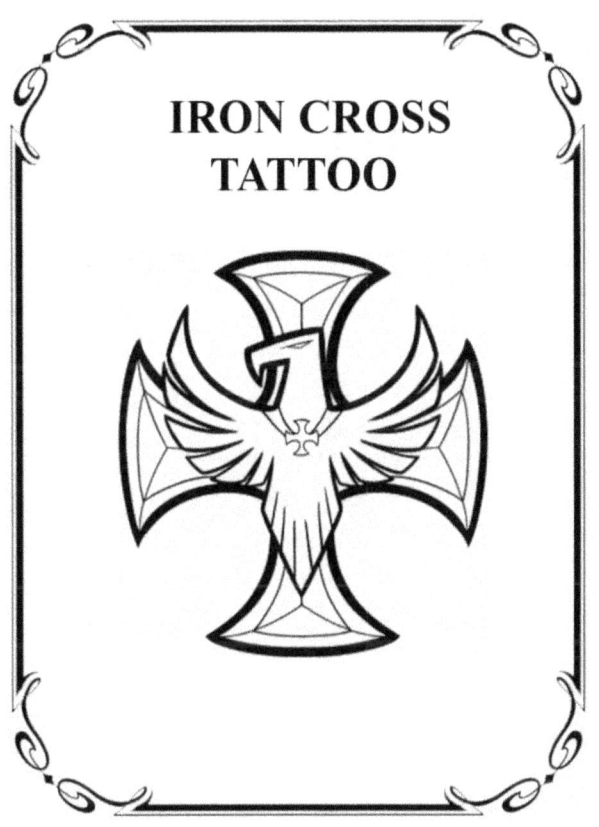

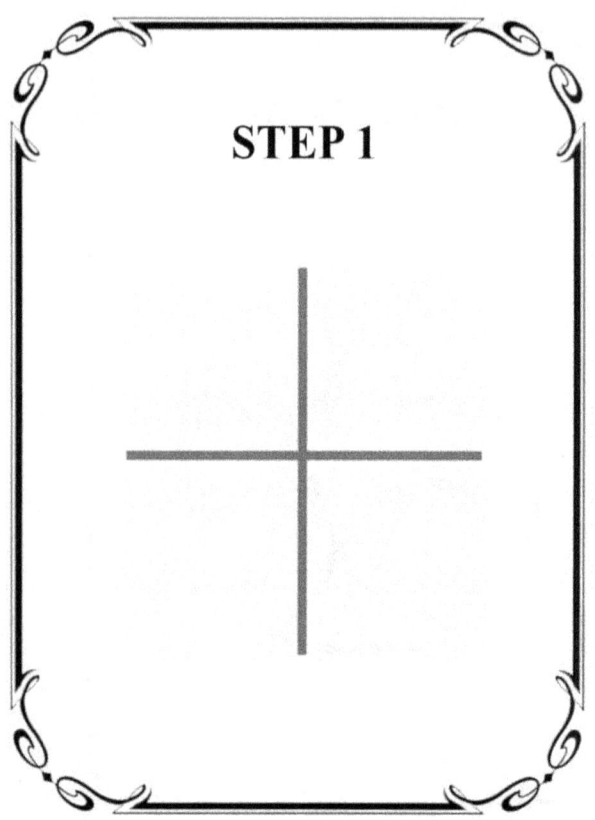

STEP 1

STEP 2

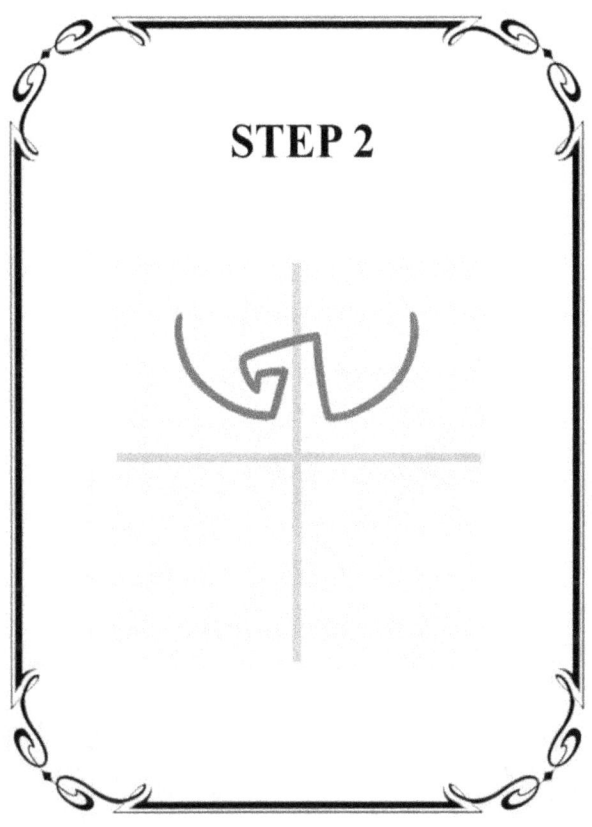

STEP 3

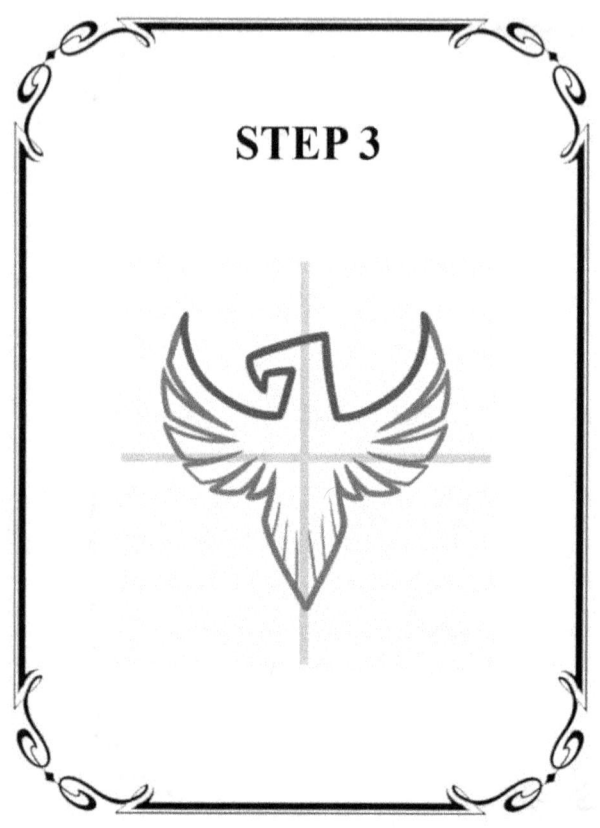

STEP 4

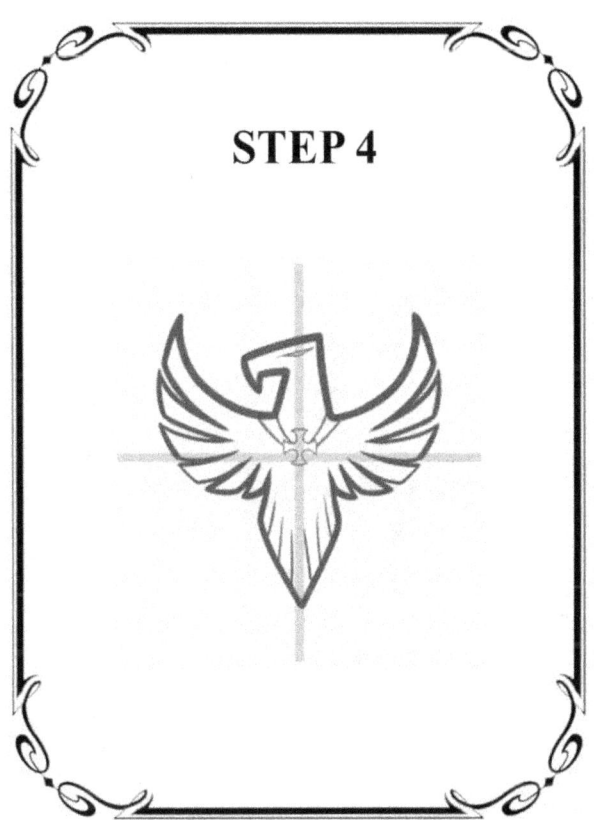

STEP 5

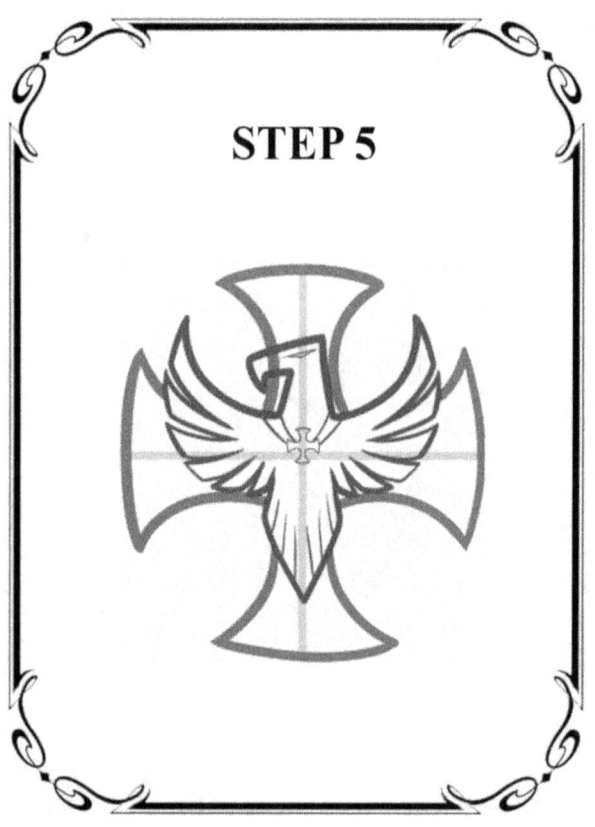

STEP 6

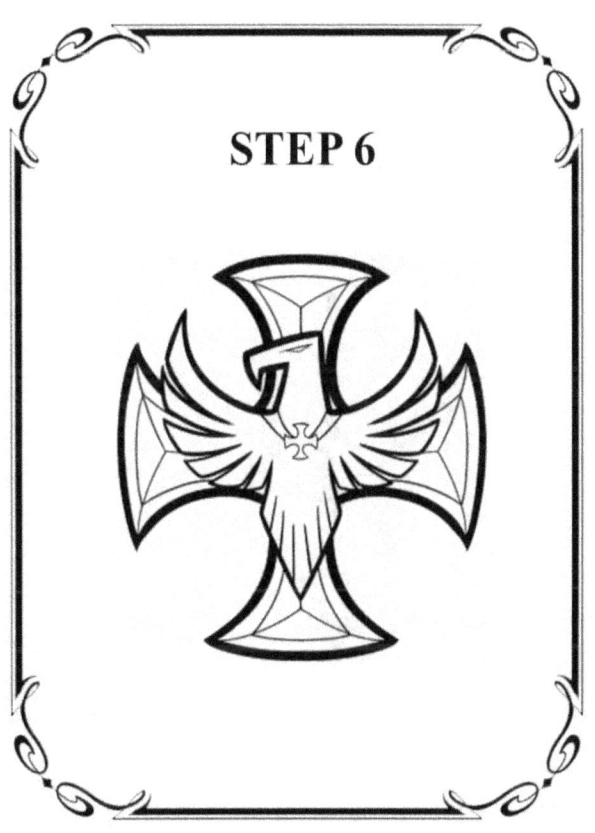

ROSE CROSS TATTOO

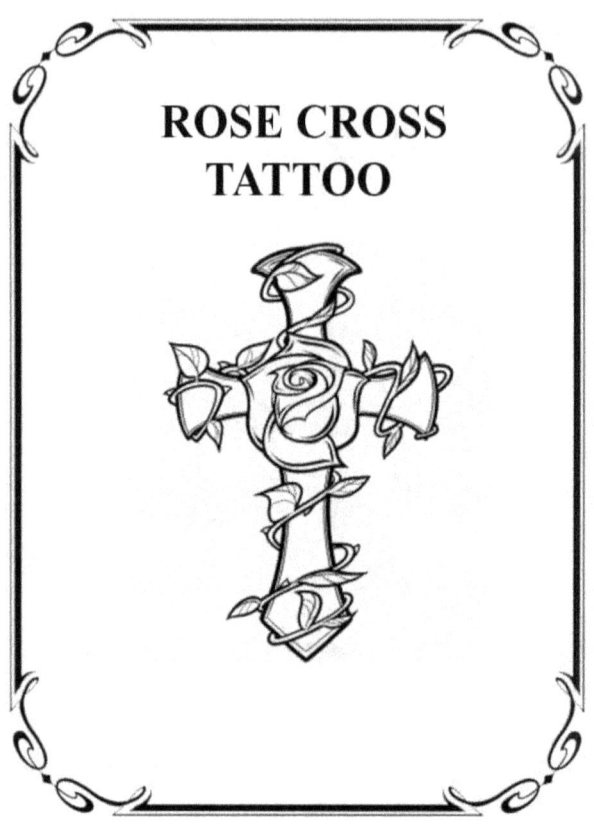

STEP 1

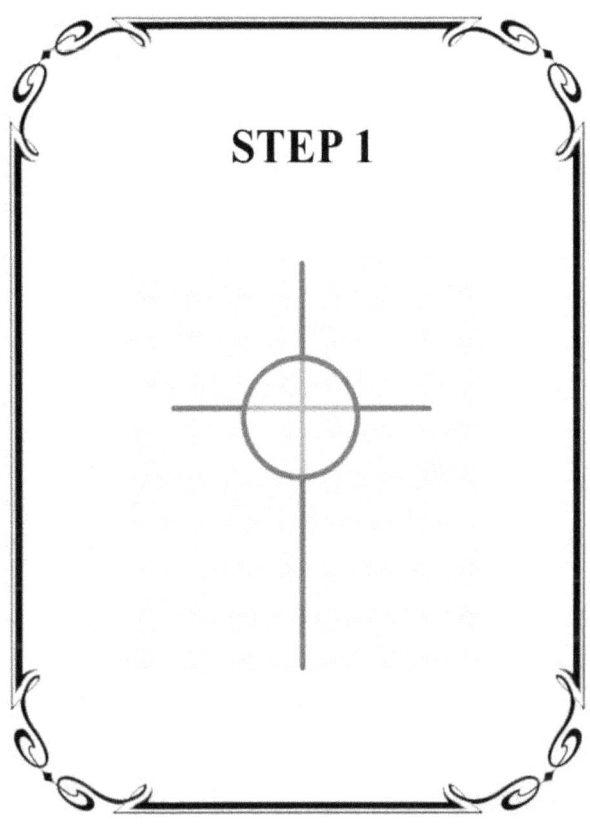

STEP 2

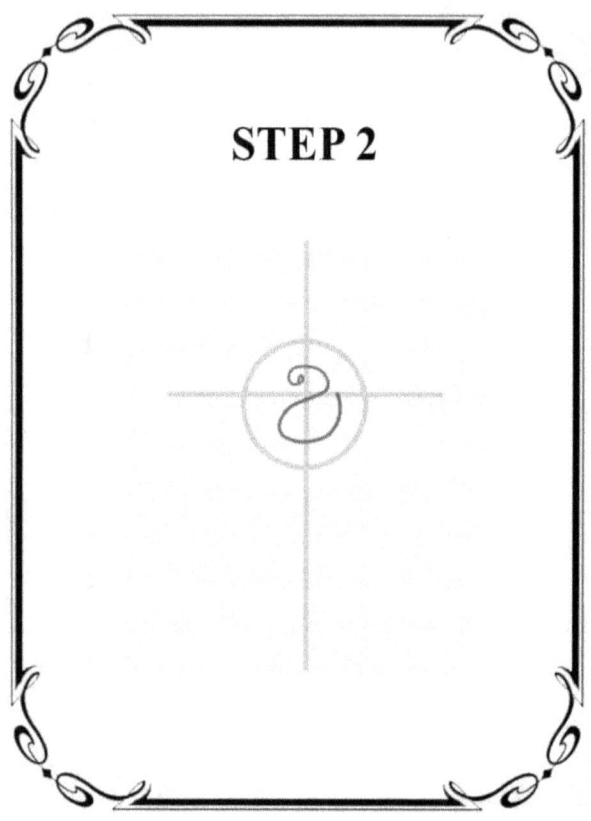

STEP 3

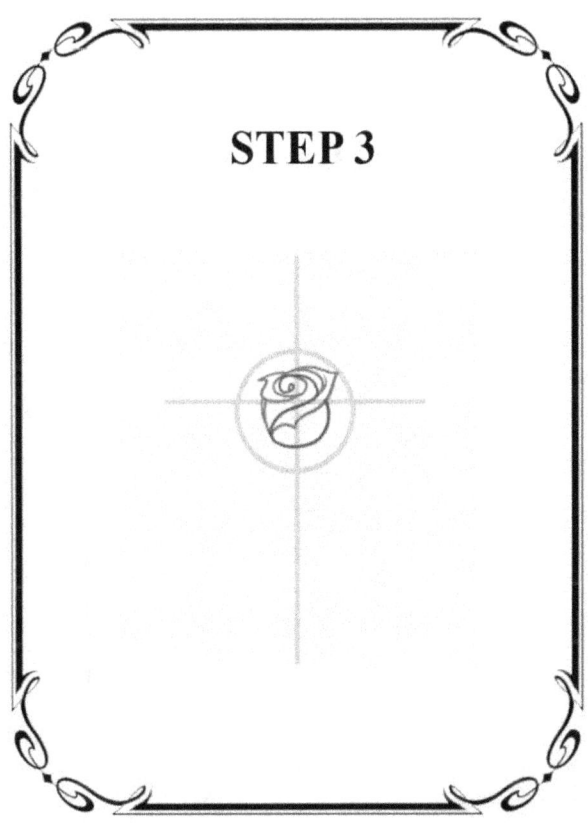

STEP 4

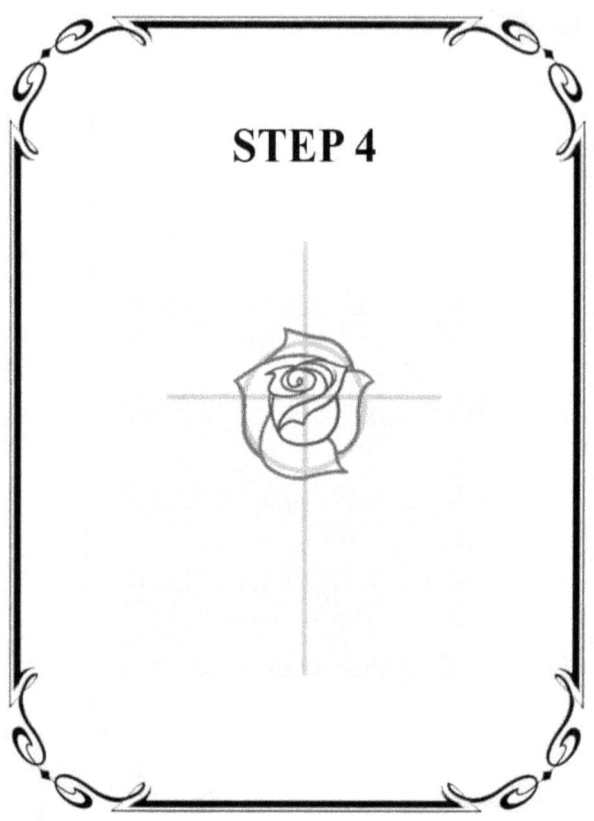

STEP 5

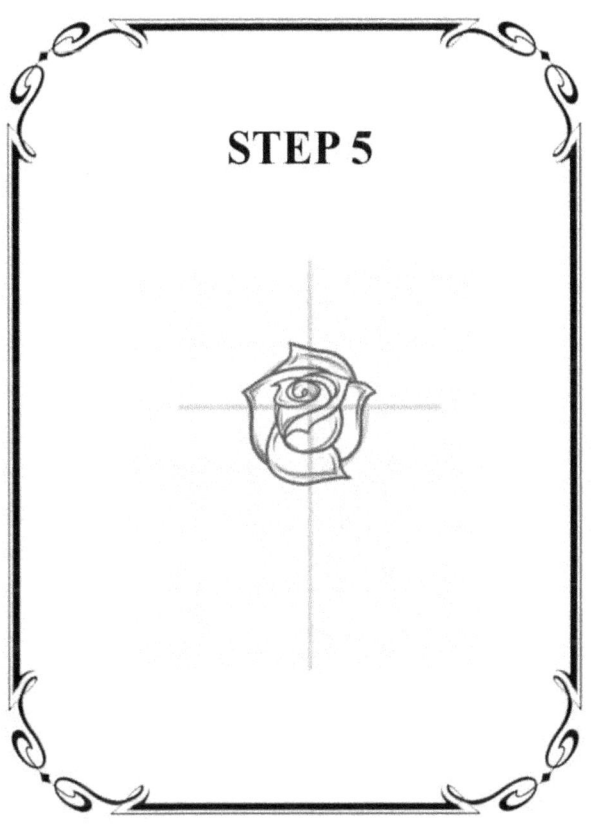

STEP 6

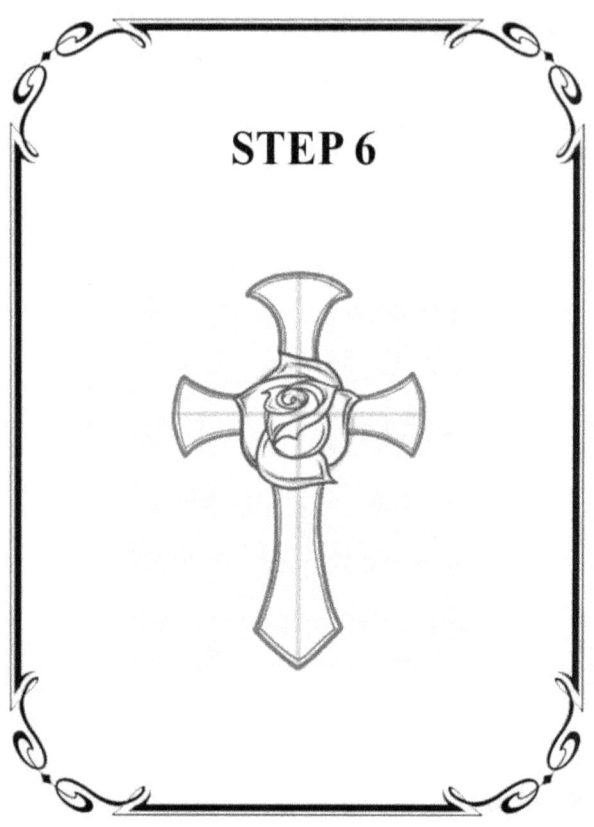

STEP 7

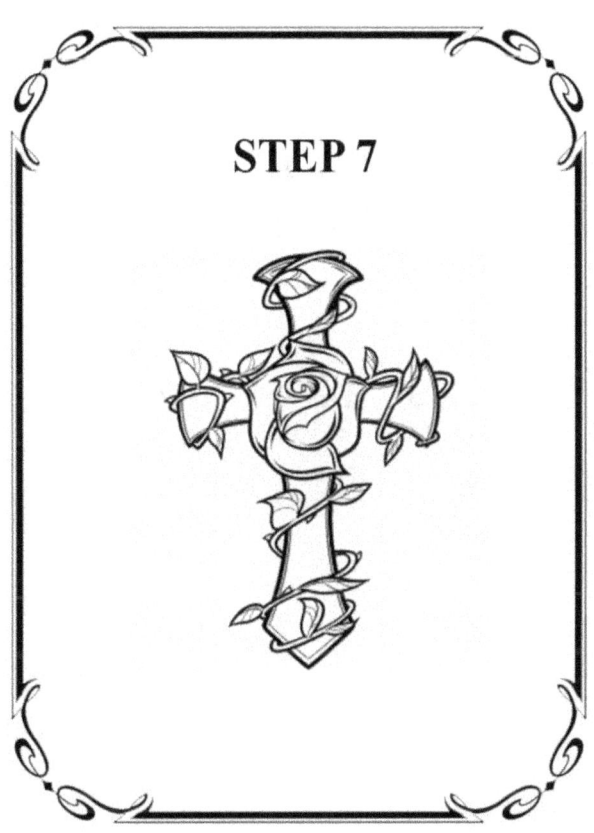

WINGED CROSS TATTOO

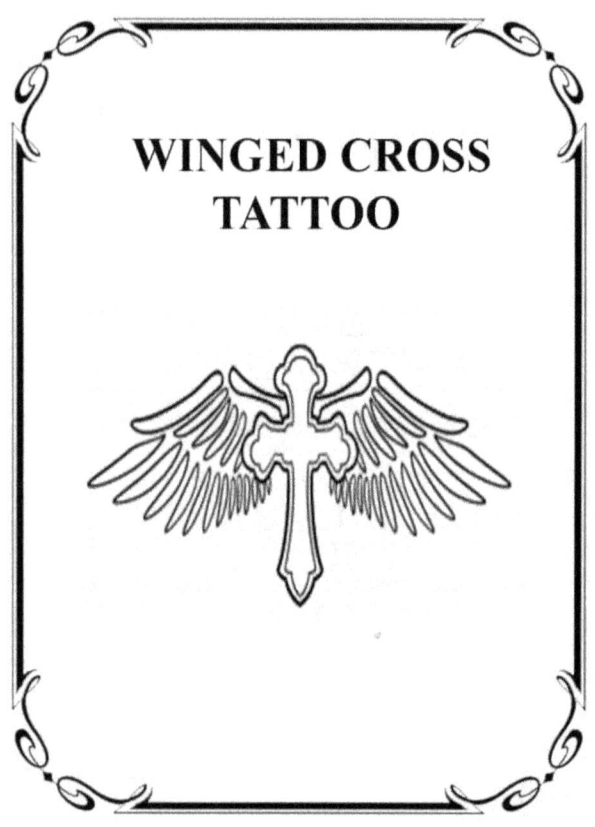

STEP 1

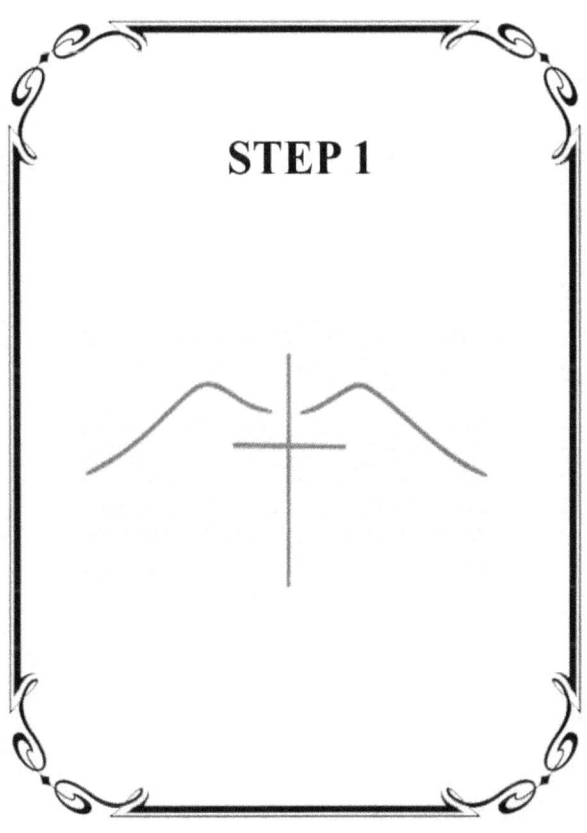

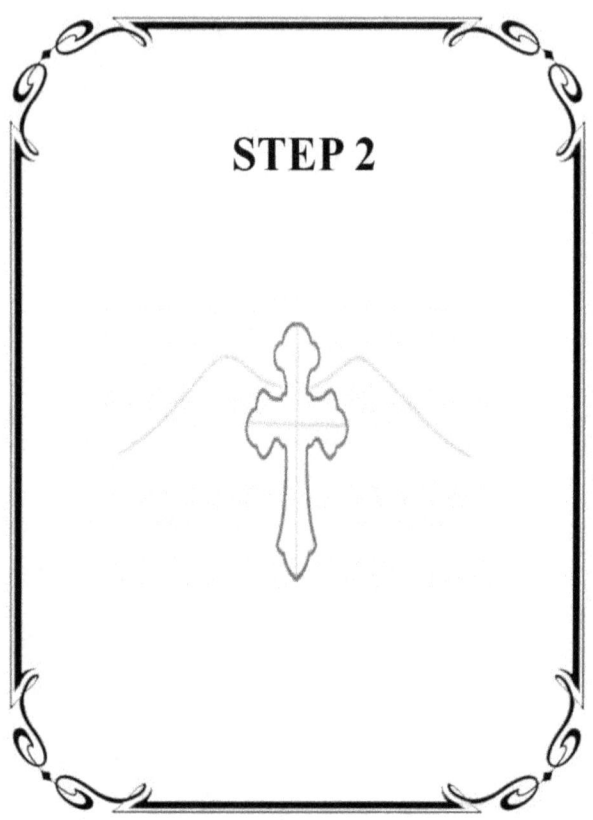

STEP 2

STEP 3

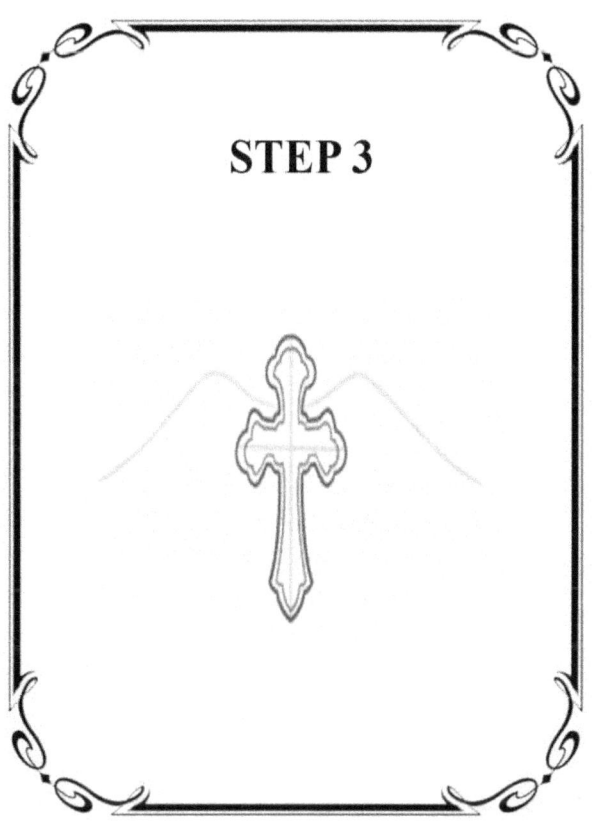

STEP 4

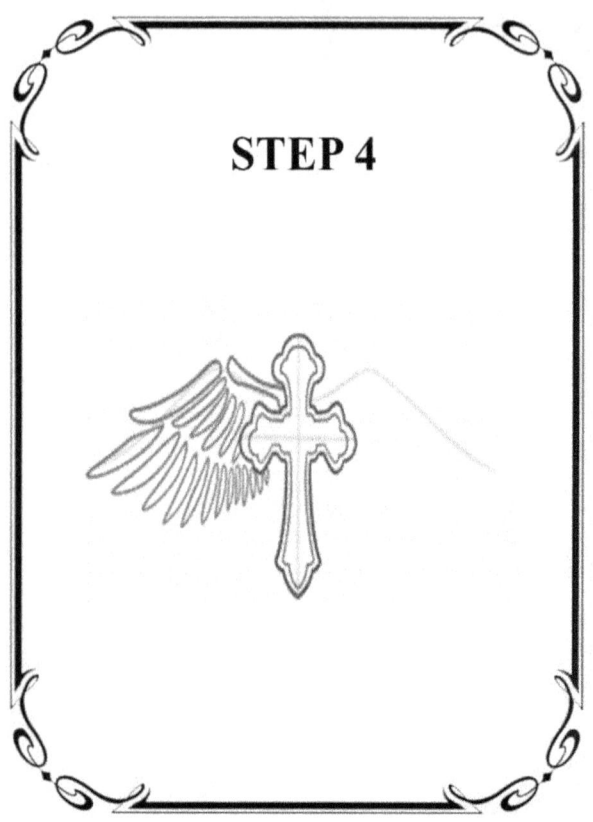

STEP 5

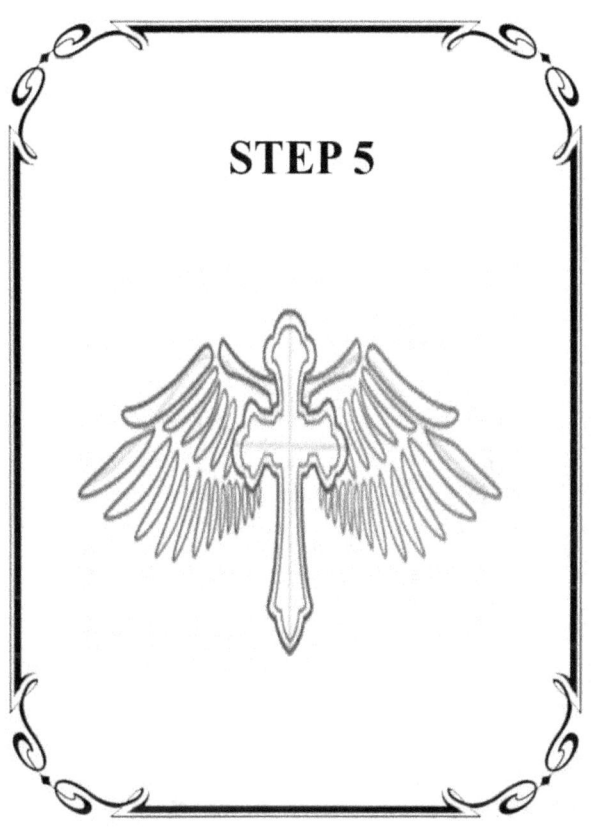

STEP 6

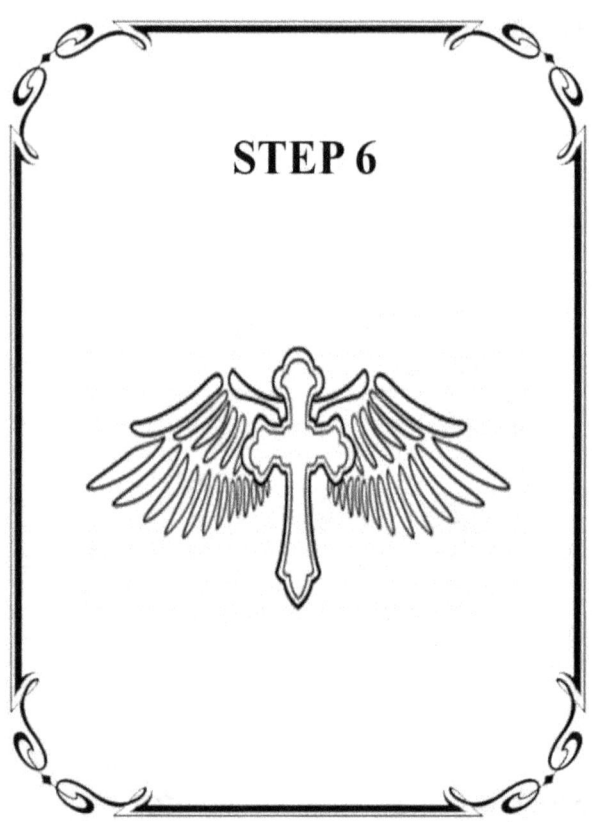

Michael Winicott

FACEBOOK: BUSINESS LESSONS FROM MARK ZUCKERBERG

Teachings from one of the most successful entrepreneurs of the world.

© 2015 by Michael Winicott.
© 2015 by UNITEXTO
All rights reserved
Published by UNITEXTO

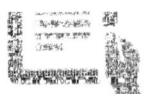